The Life After

POETRY BY MARIO SUSKO

First Journey (Sarajevo, 1965)
Second Journey or Pathos of the Mind (Zagreb, 1968)
Fantasies (Sarajevo, 1970)
Survival (Sarajevo, 1974)
Confessions (Sarajevo, 1976)
Compositions and Reflections (Sarajevo, 1977)
Land Vision (Zagreb, 1980)
Gravitations, 41 (Sarajevo, 1982)
Selected Poems (Sarajevo, 1984)
Selected Poems (Sarajevo, 1986)
Physika Meta (Rijeka, 1989)
The Book of Exodus (Tuzla, 1991)
A Handbook of Poetry (Rijeka, 1994)
Mothers, Shoes and Other Mortal Songs (Stamford, CT, 1995)
Future Past (Ljubljana, Slo., 1996)
Mothers, Shoes and Other Mortal Songs (Zagreb, 1997)
Versus Exsul (Stamford, CT, 1998)
Versus Exsul (Zagreb, 1999)
Madri, scarpe ed altre canzoni mortali (Napoli, Italy, 2001)
The Life After (Stamford, CT, 2001)

THE
LIFE
AFTER MARIO SUSKO

Yuganta
Press

Grateful acknowledgment is made to the editors of the
following magazines: *Borderlands: Texas Poetry Review*,
Bottomfish, *The Chinese Poetry International* (China), *Ellipsis*,
Fence, *Maryland Poetry Review*, *Nassau Review*, *Nuove
Lettere* (Italy), *The Onset Review*, *Poetry Emerging*, *Poetry
International*, *The Poet's Page*, *Potato Eyes*, *The Progressive*,
Seneca Review, *Sparks*, *Sulphur River Review*, *Verse*,
Wavelength, *Whiskey Island Magazine*. Also, thanks to Ramona
Cearley, Barry Fruchter, Robert Karmon, Susan Marshall,
Bruce Urquhart, Ann Yarmal, and, especially, Ralph Nazareth
for their unwavering support.

ISBN 0-938999-14-1
Library of Congress Catalog Card Number
2001 131793

First Edition

Yuganta Press
6 Rushmore Circle
Stamford, CT 06905–1029
yuganta@aol.com

For
T. M. & Z. M.
who outlived the critical mass of evil

CONTENTS

PART ONE
(minus one)

Ma perché fu sprecato tanto tempo
quando era prevedibile il risultato?

E. Montale

THE DONKEY CONNECTION

the mustiness of the wooden frame
floating slowly into my nostrils
on this humid thunder-stricken day.

within, a glassed-off man on a donkey,
his hand raised, calm and prophetic.
I'm roped off in the air-conditioned coffin.

my sweat in my mind only, no image
to be mirrored on these disposable tissues.
I think my umbrella won't protect me.

my uncle used to ride a donkey, stark
naked, a huge black umbrella hovering above
him to shield him from the mediterranean sun.

down the narrow dusty path he would
go to the end of the land, dip his feet
in the sea and mumble, no can't walk yet.

and back he went then following his donkey,
the black shadow like a jester dancing
before behind him, to paint in oil the man

that walked on water. he ended up
in jail, accused of being out of touch
with a new social order, then released

the very next day with a stack of papers
he had to have on him at all times
and sent to live in a big city inland.

don't ever do what you don't believe in,
he told me one day, gave me his papers
and rode his bike straight into a tram.

it's the donkey I keep coming back to
while trying to find my way out,
my deluded finger already on the button

that opens my bonus gift umbrella. and
as I push my bike through the driving rain,
I wonder whether I am free enough to know

I too have entered the land of my undoing.

FORLORN

The starched white cloth falling
Immaculately at the four corners
Hiding my mother's communion table
With its empire worm-furrowed legs

Waiting to be bloodied by my father
His hairy hands quartering vermilion meat
His belly laugh raining droplets of red
Wine like cherry pits I hit pigeons with

He always ate the eyes first
Of every animal head brought before him
You'll spot your enemies he would say
Grinning at me before they detect you

His belt a coiled snake on the chair
Next to him should I have failed to eat
Kidneys stomachs or hearts he had laid
Insidiously on my gold-rimmed plate

My trembling fingers tracing satin
Initials on my grandmother's bleached
Napkin which like a glazed scar tissue
Spoke of some inherited defunct nobleness

My story always the same of having fed
Ducks in the park not of having waited
Fearfully for him before a house in a strange
Part of the town till he finally came out.

I hated them both. The lonely forlorn
Boy who would pray to God at night
Kneeling on the cold waxed boards
To keep his mother and father safe

RIVER VIGIL

Whenever I asked my mother
about my father, she would say,
Your father's gone fishing.
Time and again I'd sneak out
of my bed at night and stare
at the slouching river down
in the valley. The moon would
shimmer on its ruffled skin
like a giant float with a juicy
worm from our yard in the plasma
below. I'd hear the water gurgle,
the same sound mother made
riveted to one side of her lonely
raft. And with the first wisp
of light burning the curtain
on the horizon, she'd clothe me
in my best armor, while I swayed
like a frozen branch in the wind,
and send me to stand in line
before a butcher shop for a piece
of meat. The empty hooks were
mother's arthritic fingers
that used to claw my clayey flesh
in the bomb shelter. The flies
diving at the bare counters were
Stukas in my school drawings.
I'd walk home, a meshed bag limp
in my hand, praying there be
a fat catfish with snaky barbels
in the tub, so we would all feast
under the candlelight and I would
not have to keep my vigil that night.

THOSE MARMALADE ON DARK BREAD DAYS

There it was, the twice-told tale
of killing as a way of living,
A boy with a trembling flashlight
descending once more into the basement
to see if the mousetrap his father set
held a shriveled grey hulk
with undying grin for a bite taken
and yet forever there to be eaten

All those grainy faces of dead heroes
in the past stuffed primers,
imposing heads of speakers at podiums,
flags flapping in the newsreels, white
butterfly wings he held tightly
with his twiggy fingers, a brass pin
for a dozen caught, as he stood guard
over the collective's cabbage patch

There was always some undesirable
element to be eradicated, always
some father to be emulated, a future
brighter and new, as if it could be
anything else but new, to be strived for
in those marmalade on dark bread days
when daughters of party members bloomed
under the silk blouses from some Ponte Rosso

Was it then after all those above
the waist virgins had been loved to death
secretly, teachers with rulers gone coarse
singing songs of brotherhood and unity,
birds insects and rodents exterminated
to secure classless harvests that I found
myself in the cellar with a piece of my liver
jiggling on someone's knife like marmalade:

A question to which the answer has
already been given is but a ploy, perhaps
an inviting literary maneuver, though,
I might add, often a historical need, since
that allows us to have the appearance of
progression through repetition, which is what
life invariably is: I'm alive as the redundancy
of the boy, he, as the furthering of the dead me:

GOING DOWN

I press the elevator alarm button
and hear my father's homeric laughter.

I feel his sotted breath come through
the brass mesh and pee in my pants.

The light is back on, the door opens,
and a woman with a poodle walks in.

The dog sniffs my leg and relieves himself.
The woman pulls the leash, her back

turned to me. I know her black veil
conceals my mother's beaten face.

The cage jerks and stops. She looks
at me on the way out and speaks

in my father's voice, I gave you life;
I can take it. The German shepherd

breaks away from the leash and sinks
his teeth into my arm. This is not

a real dog, I tell myself. There isn't
any pain. Tears stream down my cheeks.

A soldier dashes in. I, protection,
he yells, gives me a chocolate bar

and a chewing gum, and disappears.
The elevator drops again screechingly.

I'm in the trap space. My aunt,
dressed as mother courage, sits

in front of the wagon, smoking a pipe.
She holds a card in her left hand,

a king of spades. Don't be a coward
like your father. There will be wars

you have to die in, she sings softly,
shows me a joker and sets it aside.

Do you want me, my little one,
to tell you what your future is?

JOURNEYING

each time a train rumbles by
I am on it with my mother, she wears
dark glasses to hide a bruise
that frames her left eye, running
to my grandmother's house in a big city
before father stirs in the kingly brass bed.

the six o'clock train would stop
so often that I thought my bleary mind
conjured up the motion, and the peasants
with chickens in the baskets, whose rosy skin
was like that of my mother's breasts,
cheeses wrapped in cloth, faceless heads
without a body, and all the fragrances
blended with the sweat and the smoke,
even my mother in her blue dress,
looking out of the window at the trees
that rose ghost-like from a cotton vault.

and then I would wake up, just as the train,
snaking along the muddy river, emerged
from a tunnel and there on the slope across
loomed a dirty pink house where parentless
faces of war, their heads shiny from shaving,
their noses flattened, palms turned toward
me, dotted the window panes. and I would see
my mother's bosom heave and collapse
in a gush of words, That's where you'll go
if you turn out to be like your father.

a few days later, with my hair combed
like my father's, a huge lollipop in my hand,
we would journey back at night, past the house
that seemed to have been buried in the mountain,
until one day mother put me on the train alone,

saying, If grandma doesn't meet you, you'll find
your way to her place, right, dear, and I knew
my life as a refugee had started then and there.

THREE-POINTED STARS

two-wheeled watchdogs
snarling at the head of the column,
a black-gloved hand
rising half-way in the air
makes them fall silent,
two shiny boots stepping out
of the throbbing ebony box,
tiny puffs of dust rippling out,
the figure motions to a boy
in the rounded knot whose eyes dart
from the monocled marble
to a three-pointed star
that makes the air around dance—
wie heisst du kleine?
the hypnotic blue glass glints—
kannst du nicht sprechen?
a baton tapping the gloved palm,
the goggled specters flashing a grin—
und wo ist dein Vater?
Partisanen, ja?

the smell of food coming around
the bend, wafting across
the fields whose icing has been
clawed at by whizzing beasts
invades his raw sleep,
and the flour sky explodes above
the forest, the weightless silence
of listening till the morning,
when two white trucks
like two giant snowballs
roll into the street and he sees
himself dash through the hole
in the gaping face of the building,
his hands up in the air, eyes fixed

on a three-pointed star on the grille—
ej mali, zvat' tebia kak?
a ruddy head cranes out of the cabin—
ja pomoch. unhcr. ribnyi konzervi ljubish?
the chrome insect immobilized,
caught in the vibrating cobweb.

GOING BAD

what should I have presumed—
replenishing my refrigerator with books
when other perishable things were gone—
that their substance could be preserved
from being corrupted by time and fortune

—as a child I cracked an egg once
and in the vibrating yellow dome
there was this brownish dot
sending out filaments like red threads
that webbed my mother's eyes
when father stopped coming home—
She would only say, we don't have a box
so nothing keeps fresh for long—

But I knew she wasn't telling me the truth,
never stopped believing his seed had festered
in her, my words were not to be my deliverance

—And forty years later when the power
was cut we cooked and fried everything
on the old cylindrical stove in the cellar,
staring at words, the worms that never felt
anything, twist and cringe on sacrificial pages

—For three days we feasted unwarily,
disinherited Romans oblivious to fires
and dead bodies' stench beyond the walls

—Then there was nothing left to go bad
except us, our locution failing to move
the flies that sensed one rotted from inside—

FEAR AND MADNESS

I want to recover the moment
When I lost my mind

When my mind developed
A mind of its own.

You sat in the corner
Holding the cross between

Your palms. Bombs were falling.
I watched a triangle of white

Cloth where your legs converged.
My eyes streaming with words.

The candle on the cement floor
Making our bodies groan

On the opposite sweaty walls.
My mind twisted like the wick's

Breath. And dissipated. A rutted
Stare. You whispered. If you

Pray the fear will go away. I
Nodded. Wishing for a greater

Fear that would bring you to
Me. Then I said it. I shall be

The father of your son
Who will never know me.

BAKING BREAD

Beyond everything unreal
Nothing is the only verity

—finding a blind spot
of a mortar shell

lighting the pilot light
as the sniper's eye blinks—

Crazed calculations
Courting involuntary muscles

—as if the body could absorb
the blow and make the brain

disown the pain when the entrails
rise ethereal like batter dough

and a salty crust begins to form
on the burning shivering lips—

The mind striving in vain
To reason with the stomach

—you peer through the oven
window and there's nothing

except a hissing sound and
a fermented breathing essence

that for a moment makes you believe
there must be something beyond nothing—

But what's that got to do
With snipers and mortar shells:

Nothing if you haven't been there

TELESCOPING

I know where my dreams
sleep   in my insomnia

the light freezes   me
dancing orange yellow red

    in my mind   bees
maddened by the smoke

swarming through   the ear
drums   making the eyes

bloom   warm resinous
breath   dam the gullet

and the shadow   is flung
into the cracking hall

mirror   a warped image
    screaming   Run   Run

I moved   unmoving
a reflex   beating a firing

pin   click   already tele
scoped into a memory   dot

there is…, and there are…. and CUT
—EVERYONE KNOWS WHAT THIS IS ABOUT

there's a blade / cutting across
the bark / a thin jagged line a pen might
make / crossing out the whole sequence /

there are rays boring through the dust
and / the leafy flesh / the blade wiped
off / the tip of the pen catching a mote /

there's grass falling flat / reddened
/ slowly straightening up again / languid /
a shiny leathered palm damming a gasp

/ there's paint regurgitated / on the canvas
/ shadows extending their jellyfish hands /
the resinous sun dropping below the retina /

there's a motion in the mind /
the ribs becoming encrusted branches /
shooting into the air / gone memoryless /

and the words / on the page / that do not move
/ nerval ants strung / on the stem /
the eyes glued to the sky / that do not blink

SCALING THE SCALES

to balance a framed mind and the frameless imprints
I have to outlive by day what I can't survive by night

the curdling puddle where lumps of brain
are ruffled by the wind like crumpled larvae

the eye suddenly catching charred pieces
of clothing that hang from branches like fruit bats

the sound blow that hurls a limb up in the air
and something snaps like a twig being stepped on

after a sleepless dream all my vehicles drowned
in the tenors' silent laughter that amuses Gods

their forefinger nonchalantly on the pan to play
gravity's pull against the weight of words

and make me know the pointer's not the rider's likeness
the voice *make yourself live* is that of a ventriloquist

FUSION

Those who suffered inordinately, she says,
have the right to go round the bend willfully.

There is a legless man dancing booby-like
in his wheelchair at the empty cobbled square.

His camouflage jacket is ground zero of my gravity.
Someone is always watching, pretending not to see.

A woman with a green wig emerges, pulls up
her skirt, the ivory limbs straddle the armrests.

It is the memory, a naked vampire under the sheets,
that wraps her legs around you, eats the head.

Mantis religiosa, fixed in my drizzle glassed vision.
Someone calibrates the target, repeating the end.

I'd have to dig deep to find where your wounds
could really be, her breath ripples down my neck.

I grope for my pistol and shoot her straight
through the nipple. She stumbles back, her arms

flapping like the wings of a bird that tries
to fly away. And I fall on top of her.

The cold knife in my belly makes me see
arched colors dissipate in the veiled air.

The armored column has entered the plain,
the wheelchair I cannot get to stands empty,

a shadow of my own weight, waiting to be
rolled off by a dung beetle come daybreak.

THE LIFE OF DRECK
(or) VICE VERSA

all my sons
        flushed down the toilet
are coming back
        seeking revenge

they're the soldiers
        invading my blind corners
the wizards and chroniclers
        of the mind's mirrors and the blame

        like a dog I scour the streets
of the ravaged city
        and bark at the besieging hills
your own mothers didn't want you

        but every word of mine
becomes a fluttering moth
        that crashes back into my face
and sizzles while melting

it is too late to talk
        about what one did or did not want
as I carry my excrement
        wrapped in the glossy magazine pages

        and toss it furtively
at the corner onto the garbage mountain
        while a telescopic eye
I feel watches me gleefully

        it measures my fear
        with its mood and checks off
one day shooting particles
of my own remnants into the air

THE ACCORDION PLAYER
CONTEMPLATING SURVIVAL AND SUICIDE

Is it the ship's bassoon unseaming
the ambergris night that keeps me in check
ankle deep in this breathing void

the air expelled from the bellows
the lungs strapped voiceless with nacreous melody
keys on the shore staring at me numbly

The bride is asleep behind covered mirrors
lulled by her own moist fragrances
the groom feels his gun next to the alarm clock

his words still rustling in my ear:
if I chop off your trigger and screw you finger
how would you manage to hit the treble stop?

I have played their tunes one more time to live
one more day and take with me
two cans of mackerel and all of my fingers

To turn about and walk back into the swath
of bloody light   /   To follow the wake
aware there are no spices in the hold

WHERE I WAS

I was there   and there was   not
where I was   to be   my breath in
cised by a blast   in the brain
an imploded membrane   obliterating
the alpha   bet   beyond

the stillness   a frozen reflection
on the wall   tongueless memory
to be   where I was   to stare   at
dust particles   luminous   confetti
acidulous   in the vitreous humor

a starved child   before a soldier
a candy in the palm of his hand
the bait   taken   fifty years later
pia mater torn   a scleral marble
oblivious on the floor   there

rayless letters   trapped in the lens
where I was   and was   was not

THE SCRIPT

In the final shooting script
There was nothing resembling my mother's words,
If you start to go under, do not flail
Your hands around; let yourself go
And you'll rise back to the surface on your own.

In the small hours of the night
My bladder would swell with the amber sea
To end the thrashing drowning of a specter
That drank a single glass of water a day.

Was it fear that created all that liquid,
Or defiance, so my booted legs could navigate
Between the rocks in the gaping void,
Past the portrait on the wall that stared at
My effaced life with its bullet hollowed eyes.

In the freezing clogged bathroom
There would slowly flow this steamy yellow arc,
Creating another layer of foamy bubbles
And rings that broke up as if expiring.

And though in the time of the deadly lull
Outside any sound could have blown me away,
I would suddenly burst into laughter,
Remembering that as a child I was convinced
Those gushes from horses were my father's beer.

In the end I came to believe that in truth
I'd been made to play out my nightmare without
Knowing the script, or that someone was reading it
From the closing shot back to the opening scene.

HEADLESS

it always finds you unprepared,
though you might have seen it before,
someone has cut out your head,
a dime size hole, and your body
supports now the empty space—

you always want to know
who did it: a disenchanted lover,
tired of your self-contained smile,
your loved ones, desperate
to protect you from the enemy,
or your enemy, bent on disavowing
any past connections with you,
but in the end it doesn't matter,
your head is gone and that's it—

[I myself did a similar thing
as a child when my father left
my mother. I took her lipstick
one day and smeared his face
over and over till it got blotted out,
so in that scarred yellowish photo,
the only one that survived the war,
I hold the hand of a person
whose head is a squashed carnation.]

after a while you begin to fear
the whole thing could have started
with your mother drawing a little arrow
pointed at your pin-like head
in the first grade end-of-the-year photo—

[Years later, and by then my father's age,
I would stare at the scentless crimson clot,

trying to recover his face under it,
to see whether my features resembled his.]

yours then becomes a single-lens reflex
memory capturing semblances to throw off
the agents that are after the negatives—

LEFT BEHIND

Time to go, he says,
shoving off the last paper boat.
I watch the letters get smudged by ripples.

A solitary gull circles briefly above,
unfooled by inedible scraps.
I feel a stale piece of bread in my jacket.

He makes his way over the rocks.
Words would never have helped anyone
see why you were where you were.

I glance at the handkerchief in my hand,
a bleached pennant stained with blood,
and realize that some time back I was shot.

What I want to know is
whether it's possible to unlearn things by heart,
whether the curse of loneliness is memory.

He hurls a stone that explodes in the middle
of the decomposing flotilla. The horizon
tilts and the light slants into the crevice.

Tell me that my soul will remember
me, the words seep out, warm and sticky.
He kneels down and looks at me closely.

I am as real as you are, he says.
I have read every word of your pain,
and I'd like to believe you've felt mine as well.

He takes the bread out of my pocket
and tosses it onto the water. Through the vapor
I see the bird appear in the sky instantly.

REFRACTED

I scraped a spoonful of marmalade
Out of the jar and let it melt slowly
In my mouth, coat my parched tongue
And ooze down my throat like body fluid.

One often doesn't feel one's been shot.
The surging sensation is like a billow
Of sweetness rising through the esophagus.
The first line of a poem without words.

A bull goes down on his knees, bows
To the sounds deflating his verbless lungs.
Does he sense he gave too much of himself?
Or was brought up to mistake pain for rage?

I thrust my hand into the cloudy jar,
The raw eyes moving my tentacle fingers
Towards its sticky walls, my war refracted
Mind still fixed on two grainy prints,

Of a man lying on the sidewalk, his arms
Spread out, as if sunbathing in his Sunday
Suit, a shattered jar in a transparent bag,
Strawberry preserves imaging his entrails,

Of a matador on his toes, leaning forward,
His arm raised, a pencil like sword poised,
The scarlet cape limp, and the fighting bull,
Bloodied and spent, oblivious to his fate.

A hand always tries to dream of deflecting
A conception. I couldn't yank mine out.
I had the words, but my hand was trapped,
Betrayed by the blind witnesses of fancy.

By the time I freed myself, the sidewalk was
Empty, the estoque plunged in, the exit gate
Thrown wide open. And I couldn't remember what I
Wanted to write about. How I died, or survived.

THOSE SAVED AND THOSE SACRIFICED

—all those words that came to be
deaf and dumb in the dervish dance
of moonlit dust motes, while their tracers
drilled sizzling holes in the bookcase wall
and I was a limbless shadow flung across,
its reflex echo vaporized in every breath trough—

—still I thought if I saved the books I saved
myself, so I would climb the stairs
during the lull on a rainy and windy night,
take off my shoes and inch along the walls,
the blood whirling in the temples blindly,
my soaked shirt and the pasted paper
rubbing against each other like sweaty lovers—

What I knew, after some time, or all along,
Was that among those saved there were those
Chosen to be sacrificed, with thin soft pages
I read in the bathroom, then crumpled desolately.
Thou shalt remain, in midst of other woe
Than ours, a friend to man, to whom thou say'st,
"Beauty is truth, truth beauty,"—that is all
Ye know on earth, and all ye need to know.

But there was no beauty left in those pieces
Of broken vases that shimmered on the floor
Before me, no truth to the limbless shadow
Or the reflex echo for those across the street,
Behind the windows and the barrels, who had
A truth of their own, when I stepped out
Into the light of day, sacrificed to live.

A REVOLUTION IN THREE ACTS

                *   *   *
every line is   the final
line   before another
final line   that's how
we pretend   to forget
the edge   of pain   and
turn the page   counter
clockwise   to read on

                *   *   *
                the sum total
of flatness   must be
a revolution   that's how
we walk this earth   and
do not fall off   into
nothing   that at the end is
but the absence   of something

                *   *   *
if never again is   again
                        never
the less   of what we have
at the end of day   to be
more for some   tomorrow
is a curve   making us
journey straight   in spheres

PATTERNS OF BEING

Insects dancing above flowers
In circles, horizontally, vertically.
The intact pattern of being

Without knowing. I sit in the park
Again and wait. A book of poems
On the cement bench. A stemless red

Carnation in my hand. The redundant
Password. A girl in a white dress
Walks by cradling in her arm

A bouquet of red carnations.
In the poem she would pause, give
Me a flower and whisper, the secret

Police knows who you are. Nothing
In the end to do with a question
That precedes all. Is it through death

A forsaken man knows he conquers life,
Or the other way round. Neither
The Manifesto nor the Bible answers.

And the girl is almost out of
The park, a bobbing cotton globe
With one bloody dot on the edge.

Then she glances back, smiling
At my obsolete fantasy of man's
Ultimate purpose on earth.

The light shifts and the insects
Move to another fragrant plot.
Unwitting pilgrims of future blooms.

I open the book and read my own words,
What could their behavior bring
About but the change of colors
In the short-wave essence garden.

You'll sit in a park waiting for her
To give you a flower. She'll kiss you,
Her lipstick scentless, the gesture,
You know, conceived to betray you.

THE EAR

Virgo aurus I send to you, my Lord,
in this hand made Kenneth Cole case;
my faith I place in your just dictum,
our fate in the deeds of the ethnoparler.

To lop off one pinna, my fellow citizens,
and leave the membrane unprotected tells us
that we are all affected. Thus, I ask,
in this hour, do we not all feel ravaged?

Werra or campagne, will they come along,
if I promise them not a soul will be lost?
I can always claim we shall spielen a Krieg
with my brand new set of terra cotta figurines.

People will understand. An ear is an ear.
It is in our national interest to be all
ears to pin their ears back. Our three-deckers
are invisible to their radars in crow's nests.

Good tidings they bring, my Lord. The bellum
wasn't bello, the Porto is in ruins, but I
venture to say that we were compassionate.
And, the humanitarian aid is on the way.

We shall also, with your gracious approval,
send them other things, to show we mean well,
teddy bears, crayons, balls, generously gifted
by Toys 'r' Us; also, surplus army tents.

Others have to pitch in. My advisers tell me
our requests have fallen on deaf ears, pardon
the phrase. Oh, no one will remember the ear,
only if we contained the endemic conflicts.

And kept our ear to the ground. Trying times
are before us. Successions. Secessions. People
talk of glad bags, seeing the elephants. I
want to leave all this, go to play some golf.

PART TWO
(minus six)

Whatever is after
Is already before
Another after.

S. Marduh

It is the human that is the alien.

W. Stevens

SPANNING

each time   I blink
                   memories hunt me
a pack of relentless wild dogs
after my throat
where lungless syllables dream
of roaring
                   while they
                   their tongues stuck out
                   seem but silent
shadows
of the clouds
the wind plays with

                   this is not me
                   this is not real
                   I keep repeating
to other animals
behind the gauze
that graze on indifferently

                   my eyes are fixed
on my own shadow already overtaken
its legs up in the air
like those of my wooden horse
after I with one sweep of my hand
decided to win the battle

now if I stop
do not move and do not wink
                   will they run by and ahead
and I know
what was to happen
        will have happened
                   the glass shards in my cheeks

                    the powder odor in my nostrils
                    the light blaze in my pupils

enough to make
a hand   flip
the page

                    and
                    relegate everything to
fugue

SHELL SHOCK

sleeping   sleep plastic   flowers around   me
in the center   of a funeral   parlor   i   am
the empty air   conditioned room   this   is
lungs burn want to   get up   and out   mother
is   there   dead   out   in the rose   garden
knits me   a sweater   no sweater   summer time
take out   pocket mirror breathe   iiin   it
exit sign   reflected doesn't   doesn't blur
blazeees   worm   like in   the violet dark
nesss   the mirror   mirror   is square glass
windooow a face   there   drawn   fogs my view
scraggly its lips   move   i make out   where
to wheere   to a fool   cemmmeetery   wheeere
else   where   vanishes my mouth   full ooof
dry plaster   hands   griiip   my wrists   myyy
ankles   i aaam   carried out my head   bobbing
the world   is upside   down   stripped   walls
rock   swallow   my blood i smell   sweat   rooo
seees   put iiin   aaa car i sit   sit   a wax
doll   my hands   ooon myyy kneees   ashen   white
not   reeetouched mother   catches up   with me
my old bike   sheee's waving   myyy sweater
iiit's in her   her left hand   cold   iii'm
lungs burn   car   raaaces   shee's smaaaller
behind back   in   her arms my legs   purple
blue bounce   pain flabby   shee's tryyying
reach   the shelter's in the ground   she knows
has to pass   the guard entrance   she knows hand
goes   up   must   heilheil   mother cries criiies
siiilently my sweater   full of   holes   inhaaa
le   diiirt   mu cover her   flower   dress loo
kiiing into   her eyes   glisgliiistenniing light
flashes there   face   drawn again there   in the
glass   hiiis voice   from aaa   dissstance
sprinkles   breath   looower youuur head   a fly there

laaaands on   my twiiitwitchiing   forefffinger circles
tiiickles   my skin   awake   iii'm awake iii   aaam
theeere's mother   there   in the   garden   sits
on aaa bench   see   the sign   weeettt   paaaintt
hangs   ooon   frame   iii hear her   needles click
clickclick   sheee's theeere   is   knits aaa sweaaater

Recorded in the Military Hospital, Ward P5, on August 17,
1993, at 11:35 p.m. Patient committed suicide on August 21,
1993.

SHELL SHOCK
        (retouched)

I sleep surrounded by plastic flowers.
I am in the center of a funeral parlor.
The room is empty and air-conditioned.
My lungs burn. I want to get up and out.
My dead mother is there in the rose garden.
She's knitting me a sweater. It's summer.
I take out my pocket mirror and breathe in it.
The reflection of the exit sign does not blur.
It keeps blazing wormlike in the violet darkness.
I realize the mirror is a square glass window.
Then a drawn scraggly face fogs my view.
His lips are moving and I make out Where to.
What a fool I think. The cemetery. Where else.
The face vanishes. My mouth is full of dry plaster.

I feel hands grip my wrists and ankles.
I am being carried out. My head is bobbing.
I see the world upside down. The stripped walls rock.
I swallow my own blood. I smell sweat and roses.
I am put in a car. I sit like a wax doll.
My hands on my knees are ashen white. No retouches.
Mother catches up with me on my old bike.
She's waving the sweater in her left hand.
I'm cold. My lungs burn. The car is faster.
She is falling behind.
                        I'm back in her arms.
My blue and purple legs bounce flabbily.
She's trying to reach the shelter in the ground.
She knows she has to pass the guard at the entrance.
She knows she has to raise her hand in heil.

Mother is crying silently. My sweater is full of holes.
I inhale dirt and mud that cover her flower dress.
I look into her eyes. Glistening light flashes there.

I see the same drawn face appear in the glass square.
The voice comes from a distance. Sprinkling breath.
Don't move. We'll get you there. Lower your head.
I watch a fly land on my twitching forefinger.
It circles itself. Tickles my skin. I am awake.

I see my mother there in the garden. She sits on a bench.
I can even see a sign Wet Paint hanging on the frame.
I hear her needles clicking. She's knitting a sweater.

LIVING AND DYING

Living is, mother used to say, learning
To understand someone else's suffering.
I asked her once: is dying learning
To suffer one's own understanding?
What a clever boy you are, she said.
Then added: think of living as history,
And dying, what else but poetry.
I smiled having no idea what she meant.

I'm alive but I don't know if I could call it
Living. The game is over. There's no one around.
The theater of operations is quiet. I stare
At the dark screen waiting for my echo
To appear as a fleeting smudged dot. And
This being a poem I can also put in
A pearly moon above the south end of the pit
And a raven flopping around as if trying
To pluck it off the sky and carry it in its beak.

Am I able to understand my own suffering?
Still selfish because I'm afraid of dying?
History I know is no longer made. It's negotiated
By generals in business suits. Or businessmen
Who behave like generals. And if my life
Has been imagined history too is a virtual reality.

Poor mother, so wrong. History never had anything
To do with living. Or, so right. One comes
To learn that by suffering one's own understanding.

That is why the raven has sallied out of the poem
And fixed its spectral eye on my glassy eyeballs.

UPPER & LOWER

The small wooden box that arrived yesterday
Contains a set of my mother's teeth.

Two pink tortoise shells in the cotton snow.
Unmoving I try to make my eyes stir them

To hear the clucking they made when chewing meat.
As if the illusion could bring my mother back.

I remember seeing in documentaries camp
Survivors' mouths full of stumps and holes.

Now I look the same in the bathroom mirror.
When asked about my scars of war I smile.

So does mother. Probably. Sitting naked on
Some river bank with no plowed-over field

Across where bleached skulls come spring
Rains would plop up and grin at her ghastly.

I wonder whether she wanted to tell me
Something. That that was the way to leave

This place. Toothless. Like a baby.

THE LANGUAGE OF DREAMS

Do you dream in this language,
Someone once asked me.
I do not dream at all: I watch
A film every night with my eyes
Shut, the same shadow images
That pulsate on walls in another room.

The train clatters by, shaking my bed;
I clutch the ticket in my hand,
Sure to be the first to give it
To the conductor in this empty carriage.

And I know that will not be enough,
For someone behind him will speak out,
Dokumenten. Papers. Ausweis.

My face that runs moon-like behind
The window pane through burned-out
Houses and scrawny tree crowns
Holds its forefinger on my lips.

And I see my specter go by on a train,
Crouching under the table, a child
Once again playing hide-and-seek
With the shells that will tag my sweat,
My counted sheep already blown to bits.

One dreams in a language
That feels his pain, no more no less.

A STRAY DOG SONG

I went for a walk and barked at a dog.
He laughed at me with his tail.
I put my hand behind and wagged it.
The dog craned his neck; the owner pulled
the leash and off they went while I stood
alone in the mute night baring my teeth.

And then a dog came flying over the fence.
"This was yours, I believe," a voice said
in French. I looked at the limp body
at my bare feet and ran. Turning the corner
I saw an eyeless girl in white with a leash
in her hand. "You never tell it like it is."

I, however, kept repeating to myself, You have
to wake up. Find some excuse. The bathroom.
But the red dot twinkled on the hall wall.
And I would go on all fours, my dog taking it
as an invitation to play. Indeed, that was
the thing to do to fool death, to clown around.

The girl put the velvet leash round my neck
and said, "I will help you get out of here."
Her toothless smile was the French lieutenant's
at the frozen airport, who didn't want to know
anything about dogdom suffering. I asked her,
"With no place to go to, can one be an exile?"

She sits on the sandbags, the white disk
of her left eye beginning to rotate, red.
"Everything all right?" a voice comes out of
the dark. "Yes, officer; just taking a walk."
"Someone reported a stray dog around. Seen it?"
I shake my head, my hand reaching for my throat.

The girl dangles the leash in her bony hand.
"You are a clown," she says. "Crawling, red dots,
the lieutenant wanting some cash to fortify
his sense of power, all this is natural, and
you couldn't fool anybody. But the world needs
something to laugh at. Go now. You've been spared."

SONG OF MY DAUGHTER
(SENTIMENTAL)

when I die maybe you'll read
my poems for the first time,
trace with your fingertips
the shapes and scars of loneliness

maybe you'll understand
how vulnerable I must have been
to your hatred of my lines failing
to fend off wordy jingoists

I have not imagined my survival
which now some want me to be
an accountant of, as if life and death
were the balance of debits and credits,

which reminds me of the positive
zero some political economists talked
about not so long ago, the accessible
nothing absolving us of sins in numbers,

but where we stand in words as human
beings, the *wights*, a particle, *whit*,
and no thing, *na wiht*, on this long
journey of import doctoring and fixing

that is a different matter, given
the all-encompassing *o*, the first *nada*
which, if I closed my eyes and rearranged
the memory, could read as mere "hope"

— this then may be the reason my despair
to reclaim through words parts of you
the war has blown off meets with
your silent derision of lettermongers

SIGNS

He says he writes to forget.
Once everything is on paper
The mind will exhaust itself.

The body will not go insane
If there is no memory to play
Tricks on balance and deviation.

Nor will a soul that bleeds
Corrupt the point of its gravity.
The invisible scars their threshold.

He knows the level playing field
Of slanted targets and the margins
Made to be the measure of lost pages.

When he runs out of breath and words
Become lesions on dead skin he'll be
Exiled by his own flesh and blood.

He doesn't really see what he writes
The explosion having shaved off
One night sightless sheets of light.

What survives in those empty
Spaces is but the odor of burning
Screams. Undulating velvet ashes.

A vertical pain signifying nothing
To those who have to inherit
The wrath of recollection horizontally.

SEMBLANCES

there are four plush dogs in my room,
one in each corner, to protect me;
there are three artificial bouquets in vases,
one on my table, my desk, and my chest;
there are three cheap reproductions,
De Chirico, Chagall, Magritte, on the walls;
there is genetically altered food
in the refrigerator in the kitchenette;
there is a genuine imitation leather
couch along the living-room window;
there is my spurious wife sitting
on the couch along the living-room window;
there is a tv set facing the couch,
always on, which allows us to be off;
there is a barbed wire outside on top
of the meshed fence that shimmers in the sun—

and so on; how long could things go on like this,
if a poem imitated my own life's semblances
without forfeiting its right to self-effacement—
then perhaps a better way to see these would be:
there was a man had to bite off another man's balls,
if that could supply a dramatic element for a poem;
there was someone forced to drink his urine,
if that were not a fabricated image of evilness;
there was I burned books to bake wartime bread,
if that, found plausible, made poetry become utile—

and so on; how long could I survive in this
other world that tells me I should forget
and move on—not see a plastic bag
caught on the wire as my soul in a poem,
which the wind will eventually carry away,
or the keeper unseam, cursing under his breath—

DOUBLE TAKE

That night I dreamed of America.
When I woke up in that land twenty years
later and went to get the morning paper,
I found a dead man at my door.
The front page had my grainy photograph
and the headline read: Ethnic Strife Spreads.

I had never seen him in my life,
so I checked his pockets, found my refugee
card, my old green marble, my pen,
and a letter to my mother which began,
"I know you have always seen my father
in me...," and then realized it was him.

I stood there, not knowing what to do.
I hated that crumpled old body, still too heavy
to be dragged away from my ledged door.
There were no bullet holes, no stab wounds,
and I noticed the date on the paper,
December 17, 2013. I laughed, relieved.

Suddenly, the man groaned and looked
at me, one of his eyes not moving.
"I know you. You were in my dream,"
he said. "But I cannot remember when.
They told me to kill you, but something
happened. You vanished, or I awoke."

I took my things from him and turned.
"This is robbery," he whispered, "but I
will not say anything," not recognizing me.
I went inside, locked the door, slid the latch
into a catch, shut the bolt, put the gun
under my pillow, and continued to sleep in America.

SIMPLE LOGIC

1.

a beheaded sardine
between two slices of bread
in the people's kitchen

I swim in the ocean
searching for its head
a rooster's floats by
I eat it but am still late
for the new world order

2.
Question:
Where do refugees go?
Answer:
Certainly not to heaven.
Reason for Denial:
No one to sponsor them there.

3.

I crouch in the bushes
twisting a bird's neck
suppresssing its instinct to dart
out and betray my presence

the light trims the tongue
of leaves but I'm so close
to the earth I can smell my breath
already rotting into eternity

4.
I am tired of writing
About my survival
Dissecting dumb luck
To find some logic.

On this island I am
Supposed to be at peace
With symmetrical hedges
Indubious arrows on the pavement
And people I tell that after
Having been buried I must
Come from heaven.

Have I fulfilled the terms
Of my contract? Am I finally
Ready? Free at last,

God?

THE FORM AND THE CONTENT
OF LIVING

every delusion has its substantive variable.
—that of a goose, guarding in its nest
at the pond three perfectly normal golf balls.

which makes the counter supposition possible.
—that of dogs, behaving as if every bone buried
in that cemeterial land I left was theirs.

And yet even if I could have the golf balls
hatch in these pages and then fly off south
that for the actual goose would change nothing.

For two days later there was no trace of them.
I heard the course keeper say the whole thing
was a set-up designed by the local tv station.

So the bones will be dug out in the end to feed
the historical memory. the dogs will be corrupted
by virtually real substances. and I'll write
with inked quills surmising they'll intimate
the fowl must have felt it all had been just a show.

PROOF

[My ophthalmologist wanted to know
whether from time to time I really saw
dark blots move before me,
and I'd also wanted to ask him
about those vertical web lines,
whether I would see them too,
just as I did fluorescent green sticks
swimming like crazed bacteria
when I closed my eyes after my life
had exploded twenty feet from me,
but then he smiled gently and said
I should rest my eyes more often,
simply close them and think of nothing.]

out of the corner of my eye i catch
a spider descending from the ceiling,
a mindless pilgrim to God's gravity.

i open my book and hold it before me,
now an offering to a self-absorbed conqueror,
then slam its covers shut as hard as i can.

but there's nothing between the pages,
no twitching threads lost by the simple eye,
no recoiled smear to be scratched off when dry.

still a silvery filament sways in the light,
as if the static of my body moves it,
and i suddenly feel pedipalps feeling me.

if that's the way to survive, to make others
think you are gone, yet puzzle over
some tangible proof, i have had the wrong book.

i am a victim of letters i made to be
my dead witnesses, so i burn the book and
the spider which must be in there, somewhere.

FIGURING IT OUT

My friend told me that something stank
in my room, so I looked under my sofa,
lifted the cushions; maybe there was
a dead mouse in there; opened the closet,
took my shoes out of boxes and smelled them;
as if the dirt was rotting, he said smiling,
which made me sniff the only plant I had.
I looked behind the refrigerator, opened
every cupboard and stuck my head in;
I felt the odor too but couldn't locate it.

I know, dear reader, what you expect now,
for me to say it was I, which would tell you
that today a poet resorts, more or less, to
a prosaic fix; I will not, for that would be
an easy way out. Yet, you'll feel equally
deceived about meaning; a poem, after all,
is a kind of concrete universal, or the other
way round. Even more so if it's not a poem
about nothing. So, knowing what I was, and was not,
supposed to do, I tried to figure out what it was.

At one point I almost decided to accept
that it was I; my memories rotted in me,
of breathing in burning flesh, absorbing
with every pore the cellar's mold, feeling
a whiff of stillness go sour in my mouth.
That could certainly be an effective transfer
of one's experience. However, my friend
had told me that the thing was in the room,
which meant it was real. Then, after a while,
I said almost out loud, It was him; he farted
or his feet smelled and it was his way to

distract me. But he was gone; I was alone
and the odor was, for some reason, still there.

I mused at the end, and now you surely know,
dear reader, that the poem is nearing its
crescendo, that to know what the stench
was and where it came from was not the same
thing. My late mother visited me one night
and I asked her whether she smelled something
in my room. I am in your dream, she said;
therefore, it would make no difference,
when you wake up, whether I do or do not.
I told her I was going to put her in my poem,
but she got angry, Then when I get out of it,
she claimed, I'll be in your room too and feel
that smell you can't get rid of in your poems.

SIDE/EFFECTS

We'll have some music, she tells me,
before the reading, and asks me, her eyes
quizzing my body language, what kind
of music I'd like, something that gives
us hope, answering her own question, now
that I am here, far from the pain, the dark
forces of evil and senseless destruction
which, she believes but doesn't say it,
made me see how precious my life must be.

We do Come Sing a Song with Me; I croak
dutifully several end notes, and then I read.
I operate on myself. I let the words cut
deep, through dead cells, the dermis,
and unsheathe the muscles. Blood gushes
rhythmically from the vessels, but I am
oblivious to the torculars she seems to hold
gingerly in her hands. I know all about blunt
hooks, jaws and sequestrum forceps, but I
want to get to the bone, holding the ligature
tightly with my forefingers and thumbs
that will noose and strangulate the tumor.

I close the pit and the woman offers me
tissue to wipe my forehead. A chair creaks,
scraping my skin; a small hunched man
walks to a long table which I now see
along the right wall, with coffee and tea
pots, sandwiches meticulously stacked,
pyramids of smoked meats, paper plates
with cookies of all colors, several cheese
platters, each hemmed by a band of grapes,
leftover christmas napkins, paper cups,
and rows of aptly arranged plastic knives.

It was so beautiful, the woman whispers;
you must come again, and I know she doesn't
mean it. Her body got smaller, her face
is gaunt, eyes jaundiced and depressed.
Before I leave, I tell her, You've guessed,
probably, it is the human that is the alien.
Is that a new poem, she asks. I smile,
feeling the curdled blood under my tongue.

A LECTURE
IN THE SENIOR ADULT DEPARTMENT

They came two floors down,
shadows choosing their seats carefully,
having left for a moment their bingo game
and a discussion about next week's dance classes.

I talked about willful destruction,
a university teacher playing soccer
with a human head, people jumping
into the open grave to hide from shrapnel.

I was not telling them anything new.
It was an old story well retold.
A woman in the front row
with a green and yellow hat,
small slipper shoes on invisible feet,
had her eyes closed, her mouth half-open,
head tilted back, as if she were dead
while sleeping, or asleep while dying,
I didn't know. And I wanted to know
whether she was absent from my suffering,
or whether I couldn't comprehend
her refusal to feel pain once again.

When I was through
and the polite applause filled the room,
she opened her eyes and said,
"I lost all my family," her voice seeping
into my consciousness which had removed me
from counting how many candles I had lit,
"at Bergen-Belsen. Have you been there?
You look old enough to have been there.
Schlecht place that was, schlecht."

She got up and shuffled out,
swaying like some overblown flower
in the gentle summer breeze.
A man in the back smiled, turning
a walking-stick umbrella between his legs,
and said, "Edith is something else.
She always asks this question
when someone talks about these things."

Back upstairs to get my honorarium,
I saw her playing bingo.
I waved to her when she raised her eyes
and looked at the check in my hand,
my proof that I was still alive, perhaps.
Then someone called a number
and she smiled at me as if letting me
know the first dance next week was mine.

AUTOBIOGRAPHICAL

I

mother would say when I spoke
of America, Don't you get carried away;
that place is not for a soul like yours.
it'll be a beautiful, yet plastic rose.

I was, however, tired of those black-
and-white Italian movies she took me to,
those stone houses, the dust, the dirt,
the goats, and bony dogs, men sitting
along the church projection like a string
of crows, shoutings and misplaced revolts
that ended up in wind-swept cemeteries,
hungry kids that stood, barefoot, rheumy,
at the threshold, waving to their father
who with a piece of bread and cheese
wrapped in a soiled cloth was going away
to that promised land over the horizon.

I never saw any of those sun-furrowed men
again in an American movie, but it didn't
matter much to me; I knew they all lived
in huge houses with a floor in the kitchen
that sparkled like virginal snow, large
windows overlooking the crystal blue sea,
the curtains breathing with a piny breeze,
while they, clean-shaven, scented, listened
to Lanza's voice permeate their soul.
This is just a movie, my mother would say;
of those others, This reaches your nostrils.
she lived the neorealism of our own existence.

I, the past's future. my wife was to be
Ava Gardner; true, I knew nothing of Frank

Sinatra, nor would I have cared. the movies
I watched were several years old, anyway.

                    II
You are where you are, she wrote, exiled
to pictures and mirrors in which you see
what you'd have to forget to remember.
would you be able to smell your soul then?

I have a beautiful house, I would write back,
each time adding another cinemascopic detail,
with two bathrooms you can almost dance in;
no quarreling over the needs, no banging
on the door. at night I sit on the porch,
no rumbling sounds of tracks coming pertly
around the bend, slick clickings of cocking
levers to jar my ears or even memories. I
take a walk to the moonlit beach, unafraid
I am a moth already caught in a reticle.

All my letters to her ended the same way,
You must get well soon and come to see me;
yet, I prayed she would die before she asked
for some proof I didn't live one of my movies.

THREE SISTERS

Could I find some solace in thinking
they are free of dying?
I look for a country where I would lay them
to rest. Each of them has perished
alone in a different universe.

Do I feel anger or pain,
a young boy peering at the border
no more, who dwelt in their magic world
of tragedy and comedy, believing
he would be purged, sing a song
and laugh his head off?

I watched them take off their wigs,
peel off false eyelashes,
smear their face with vaseline
to remove their stage skin.
Would I have seen they lied to themselves
and thus to me as well?

What I saw was what I imagined,
and that was the truth, even when I had
to act it out, fatherless and loveless,
be a Gerard Philipe as Cid, or a doctor
in a plague ridden Mexican village
drinking his soul to death,

yet know those breathing walls
were to be rolled up at the end
and reveal a blank cyclorama
facing the ghostly glow from the prompt
box, the only sound that of a fly man
pulling the lines like bell-ropes.

Those retracting blades, poison sugar
slipped into champagne glasses,
ducats whose gold stained my fingers
if I held them too long, I knew
them all, my two aunts, my mother,
who died so many times in this other

life and then rose again to bow
with the living. They can't be gone
now. I'll just wait for them to change,
appear from behind the screen,
and we'll walk home with the word *fine*
blazing on our backs till tomorrow.

THREE-QUARTER TIME

Time is a dream in which I dance
with my dead mother, breathless,
the same way she whirled me as a child
around the half-empty room,
grabbing me by my skinny wrists,
and I caught glimpses of the gaping closet
where my father's things used to be.
We are on the wispy cotton floor
superimposed upon the ceiling of the hall,
the invisible orchestra playing for encore
"Am Schöne Blau Donau."

She knows nothing now about the corpses
that turned almost endlessly in the middle
of the river, then, flung out, bobbed
on the muddy waves, their arms stretched out
as if looking for another partner;
or about the day father pushed my head
beneath the surface, chanting mockingly
one-two-three one-two-three, then plucked
me out grinning and whispered into my ear,
"Learn to hold your breath, and your tongue,
you little river rat. You saw nothing."

Does she think as long as we dance I'll stay
alive; I'll never wake up to remember
the time when after the beatings I had
to stand dead silent facing the wall
that cried for me; or when I found myself
near the bridge and dared not cross it
to look for her behind the barbed wire,
her suitcase packed, filled with photographs,
papers, recipes, old prescriptions, warm
clothes, all useless because neither she nor I,
living one-quarter time, was going anywhere.

So we dance now, and she keeps squeaking softly,
"Forever the river will flow,
you'll be back tomorrow,"
and I keep thinking, while her eyes are closed
and she calls me by my father's name,
I've learned to hold my tongue,
learned to hold my breath.

BLIND WALK

The glass doors open with a jerk.
I start to walk. I try not to think.
My head is tilted, as if avoiding
a blow. The surge of blood
pushing my thoughts against the right
wall of the skull. There's a drum
in my temple, armless pounding.
Time is jammed in this raw
membrane of voiceless rhythms.
An unfinished sentence. A child
dragged by his mother keeps glancing
at me, then sticks his blue tongue
out. My mind goes through the same
motion my lips turn into a smile.
I want his mother to look at me.
Are we both from the same city?
Did we stand in the same mute line
for a blanket or a bucket of water?
Are we both alive in this sterile
corridor flanked by Remy Martin
and Rado ads because we didn't know
better? Already overtaken by
a group of young men, laughing and
jostling, with duty free bags in
their hands, muzzled cameras slung
over their shoulders. A horse-faced
old man with a unicef bag, a toy gun
barrel protruding out, catches up
with her and like an animal sensing
the approach she turns, her eyes
white like two hard boiled eggs.
He motions to me to move past them.
I hear him whisper, Do you know
who's here…? I strain my ears.
It's him, I tell you… The poet.

I quicken my pace and turning
the corner I look at the kid again.
The same blue tongue now blows
a huge pink bubble that goes bang.
His mother's head jerks slightly.
Will he reappear ten years from
now to put me down? Knowing
that I will be in some corridor
moving like a bat caught in
the blinding unechoing light.

LIFE. LISTED ALPHABETICALLY.

At the end of this island
I closed the book and buried
my own shadow. The sun's agent
came to me and said calmly,
What is this masquerade all about?
We know who you are.
We know your size, your reach.

What was I then to be afraid of—
The length or the weight of my pain,
The life at war with page numbers—
I held my breath time and again,
swept my footprints with a besom.
The memory carried across the ocean
is now a growth rising in my belly.

They dug me out one day and put
me on the table to dry, a shadow-
free lamp drilling holes in my eyes.
A sightless child caught in
the shimmering crystal ray, tearing
pages out of the book and letting
them fly—letters, life, light.

No visible traumas, the paper read.
You could have profited from the thing,
the agent said. Truth is a variable.
It will seldom be listed alphabetically.
And that's something you were not able
to comprehend. What you put in the ground
is chimeric because it does not end

where you end. He gave me a copy
of the revised edition, took off
his shoes and made me put them on.

I stood there, motionless, and watched
a child trying to stamp his shadow
in the sand. His mother, a refugee
like me, waded slowly into the water.

Unmoved I followed her, repeating
to myself obliviously. She can't vanish.
Like everything else this is just a tale.

THE STORY OF HATE

in time I'd have to be out of time
to forget / the present in the past
tense — digging up one's life, knowing
one gets to the cancellous dust /
the words that are singular periods
— time's jesters in the space of plotted
revolutions / healing which comes to be
peeling the skin to efface the lesions /

if that be another delusion about out-
living — grandmother putting the blanket
over her head, as if to measure her pulse
against that of the magic eye / whispering,
az a leyb shloft, lozt men im shlof'n /
while the antenna sniffed the evening air
like a cold-blooded hound / her time
of release was already a tetanized memory /

animals are different now — in these
exiled words / my dogs lie — sleeping
with their eyes open / they play hide-
and-seek with my unforgiving wake / and
sense that when the bones are dug out
my hate will make my pain hate me /

MIRRORS

aiming mirrors at the sun, she
says, will not tell you when your sanity
will leave you; her ankles dangle
in the water, and I try to conjure up
some big fish to gauge her fear.

she is quicker: I still see the glass,
small triangles tweezed out of your flesh,
colored by the candle's wavering flame,
a droplet of blood racing after a drop
of sweat, your eyes deflecting explosions.

she strikes a match; its head flies off,
a tailless spermatozoon that lands in my hair.
I do not move; she laughs: your mirror
is on fire. I watch my featureless reflection
on the glazed surface extend towards the horizon.

your own survival frightens you, she
yells suddenly and pushes me in. I fall into
my own shadow, blowing out the refracted rays.
her feet are gone; I hear my heart billow
in my ears and swim away from myself.

she tilts the cheval glass, and my body
rises to the ceiling, my image eyeless
in her belly. will you ever come back, she
asks, as I drag the mirror onto the balcony;
I aim it at the sun that hangs on a silkworm
wire, sensing the electric calm around,
the coming of a shadowless great white.

(FRIED NERVES:) SOUNDS

There is a sound in my brain
when I keep my eyes closed, its pitch
getting higher and higher, so I
wake up, wishing I could get it
out like a magician that pulls
a thread out of his grinning mouth
with shining needles strung on neatly.

I used to whistle beautiful songs,
Modugno's, Endrigo's, but I cannot
do that any more. Only a hissing sound
comes out, the kind my grandfather
would make when he got back home
from his throat cancer operation.
Sometimes I would almost chuckle
after he tried to tell me something,
those sszzzs and eeezs becoming shriller,
turning into a manic whistling kettle.

I am back in a hotel, in bed, having
scraped six months of dirt, watched
it being sucked by a tub gullet;
I aborted myself, but I cannot
fall asleep, after eighteen hours
of crawling, running, walking, flying,
because there's no sound of shells,
machine guns, just a distant hum
of electric wires. Silence has become
my torturous clang, my passing bell.

In another world after, where cancer
does not come from stress, fried
nerves as my mother used to say,
or the shortcircuited mind, so I
often thought when young it was

a form of madness, but from the walls,
cigarettes (grandfather never smoked),
chemicals claiming innocence
on food packages, I hear the tone color
of the sun flare, cutting my breath,
making me see my head explode
like a watermelon shot by a sniper
at the market place, its watery
pulp landing on my faded shirt,
as if a painter splashed his canvas red,
while I, my ears blinded by screams,
tried rabidly to pluck off black pits
suddenly turned frantic shellacked ticks.

Sound waves eating my nerve fibers
in the pons, making my head bob,
that of a rag doll, as I press it against
the pillow, pulling the unending invisible
suture out of my throat, the needles
twinkling, the intermittent cell current
that blares in my grandfather eyeballs.

RELEASE

Today I have not woken up.
I saw the maid come in
with a pile of clean white
towels and go stiff, her body
leaning back, drop them onto
the floor and run out.
I tried to imagine how I
looked, my mouth half
open, my head off the side
of the bed, my hand hanging
palm up, scooping the air.
I gazed at the world upside
down. A woman on the tv
screen mouthed words im-
passively, the picture showing
dead bodies in the icy field
behind my invisible house.

It was so relieving to be
far from the madness—deaf
in a peaceful hotel, waiting
for the maid to come back
with a manager, which she did,
stood above me close enough
for me to see up her alabaster
legs and let my head crawl
between them, her fingers
trying in vain to straighten
her skirt, while the picture
on the screen bounced, apcs
too, going through the empty
streets, the smoke running
into the sky down, a cow
holding onto the ground

ceiling, and all that damn
business of containing life.

She lifted my head gently
onto the pillow, her palms
cold and sandy, my eyes
almost touching her nipples,
two protruding buds ready
to explode in the lidded light,
and for a moment only I caught
my face in the mirror, a smile
of release on my milky lips.

FINALE

shall I be there, again,
to tell you that nothing happened,
that time will heal all wounds,
and let you look into my eyes
where the only visible scars are—

and if I come back, will I
have to leap out of myself again,
forced to perform one more salto
mortale, while the audience stands
at ease, knowing how the act ends—

a passing glimpse of the master
of ceremony, his whip hand raised,
the whistle, suspended in the brain
after the cockle stairs burst,
sucking the oxygen out of the cells—

if the body kneels, does the mind
keep standing up, fighting gravity,
there where words are rotting
apples on the ground, memory
but a seedless weight in the loins—

if the greatest pain becomes
the one not felt, and *they who have
no arms have cleanest hands*, the ring
is a scale pan of the corrupted rider,
I'm an error in the order of appearance—

then the right moment must have come
for those with a bucket and a mop to step
in, pretending to corner a circle in
a circle, and sweep the blood light,
the finale procession poised in the wings—

if these words are to go out with me,
having missed the curve of a trajectory
while I was tracing the circumference
of a dot, I am a witness of the plumb
balance who has not survived himself—

CHOICES

were I not to go I would have to fall
silent or talk like a deranged sayer
(how close is close to a wall
at seventy miles per hour if the answer
is faster than the question) to know
I do not choose what has already chosen me.

when after the war I was infested
with round worms, mother would put
the exorcising potion before me, a cup
of steaming milk with sugar and crushed
garlic in it, and say, Bottoms up,
If you do not want those devils
To crawl out through your mouth.
the next day I'd sit for hours
in the cold outhouse, both my hands
over my sealed lips, praying
with my eyes they do not choose
the wrong way to leave my body.

unloved because still alive,
unable to love because by now gone,
with keys in my hand, yet homeless,
my pockets full of tablets my false teeth
cannot bite into (my own transparent
face looks at me in my sleep and asks,
Do you think words could worm your mind),
my survival a joke for a squirrel I feed
that has to cross the road every day
to get to its home tree in the yard
patrolled by a spotted cat, I am left
with the overrun memory to the curve of chance.

SEARCHING FOR DEAD MOTHER

I will (if I) live long enough
to see myself, a lost but driven
man, walk among the uneven mounds
in the land of leavened epics—

followed by a dog (there's always
a designated mongrel in places like these)
that tracks the stirring of bones freed
from the rotted coffins in the realm below—

then following him (when he lifts his leg,
I wait for him to mark the right spot),
I come to think (once the motion becomes
just that) I'll be where my mother is—

but he seems to have an endless supply
of squirts, and I, a limited amount of time
to find her and not be found (could all this
end if I grab a stone, ready to strike—

one of us then has to wake up, somewhere,
if I tear the pages out of history books,
rewrite my mother's fate) before the gate closes
and I have to return in yet another life again—

RECONSTRUCTION

Mother will sit at the table
in the cold white kitchen,
waiting for me to bring her
my book in which I write
how I dug up her bones
to take them back home.

She'll be there, reconstructed,
like the faces of the houses,
with me wondering which tree
in the park that will never sprout
twigs again was her coffin.

My hand will smell of dirt
and rotten leaves as I turn
the pages looking for some proof
which is not a painted-over truth.
Knowing where she truly is perhaps
I'd forget where I must be.

She'll say, I've never understood
any of your poems, and I'll see myself
closing the book gently in her lap,
pretending I have the wrong page,
the wrong house, and the wrong city.

THE LIFE AFTER

is:

a probe coming in contact
with your pulp open and wide

a heat-seeking afterimage
tagging the home base

a mind moored in the ruins
its repeaters talking to the dead

papers endlessly duplicating
who you are when you are no more

the bones artificially flavored
read by vegetarian witchdoctors

your shadow at the intersection
waiting for the light to cross over

the life
after is the life

after

CODA

the life
        after
                is

                before
the life
        before

                is
the life
        after

ADD/END/um

When his daughter called and told me that she had found Mario's manuscript and papers among her father's things, I was at first surprised, then almost annoyed. I knew I was not going to resist the temptation not to check them, though I must admit that I was, by then, a bit tired of retrieving and sorting out Mario's papers. There were several reasons for that. I had myself started to dabble in poetry, so to go back to the material I thought had been exhausted meant to play a poetic butler again. Furthermore, I did not want to dig one more time into my own notes about and conversations with Mario, perhaps because I would be confronted with the old question of writing more substantially about him or detaching myself completely from the often painful sojourn through his life and poetry. But, curiosity got the better of me, especially when Nazareth's daughter mentioned that there were her father's notes and correspondence among those effects as well. Some of Nazareth's papers are copies of letters to people in which he tries to help Mario gain a foothold in this "new" environment. One of them reads, "I feel that unless something remarkable happens, he will continue to lack the kind of acknowledgment which I believe he deserves. In this regard, I was wondering if you might have some concrete suggestions as to how we may try to promote his work, including possibly the names of well-known literary figures who might be interested and generous enough to give it a push and bring it into the limelight." Most of the letters carry a hand-written comment, "No response."

The manuscript itself was paginated, though some of the poems were obviously shuffled (by Mario or Nazareth?); some of them were typed together with longhand copies, some not. (Incidentally, there were several hand-copied poems from the previous manuscript, which Mario no doubt considered to be contextually relevant.) Many poems had the poet's notes on the margins, some Nazareth's, including the latter's slips of paper inserted among the pages. It became increasingly interesting for me to try to compare some papers which I had with Nazareth's notes and remarks. It is quite clear that Nazareth knew most of the poems outside their manuscript form; his notes are sometimes part of a "dialogue" with the poet. For instance, with regard to "Three-Quarter Time," Nazareth's note reads, "I've suggested to Mario that 'cottony floor' is too 'light' a solution to what he wants to convey, the old black-and-white TV picture of the Wien phil-harmonic New Year's concert, when dancers were projected on the ceiling of the hall together with the clouds that they supposedly danced on. He has changed the line to read 'wispy cotton floor,' adding also 'superimposed' (the word I dislike utterly) 'upon the ceiling of the hall.' His explana-tion is that he wanted to create the clouds-as-cotton image ('wispy?'). Mario is simply too fond of adjectives. I told him that poetry here didn't go for an abundant use of modifiers; they are considered to be somewhat old-fashioned tools. His response was that a noun without an adjective was often like a person without clothes—naked and dull. What can I say?" In the poem "Choices" the final line read "with the curved memory to the choice of chance," where the word "curved" was crossed out and "overrun" added; the word "choice" was deleted, and underneath there were two words with a question mark, "path" and "curve." Nazareth circled the word "curve" and wrote on the margin, "Use this." Some-times he made the choice on his own, as in "Side/Effects," changing the word "flesh" into "meats" in the line "pyramids of smoked meats."

It is clear that Mario was very particular about detailed image type scenes. He told me once, "When you go through a war, you often become acutely focused on isolated pic-tures, frames, so to speak, where one detail, or several details, combined with some memory trigger element, forms an indi-rect relationship." I remember we were eating lunch one day. I had a fancy magazine next to me which he stared at for a long time. "Do you know I ended up wiping my ass with pages like these?" he said suddenly. "Can you imagine how hard that is, with these glossy pages?" I thought his question, given the milieu, was almost inappropriate. But, this was that trigger element creating possible poetic associations. "I should write a poem about that," he added and laughed. He proceeded to tell me that during the war he ran out of all possible paper, and then he remembered that he had stored in his mother-in-law's basement boxes of magazines, McCall's, House and Garden, and others, he subscribed to while living in this country. So he used those magazines; also, to carry his excrement when the toilet clogged and froze and throw it on a huge pile of garbage in the street. "Empty military rations, mackerel tins and my shit," he said with a smile. "It was winter, and I didn't think I was going to live till summer to have that odor come back to me." I never thought about the mental anguish and possible real or absurd connotations something like that could carry until I read "The Life of Dreck."

Towards the end he was extremely reluctant to talk about things that had happened to him. "It's pointless," he would say. "People are already indifferent to these things. I sometimes question myself, 'Do I overdo it? Do I try to create something that in this world is such a commonplace by now that it simply does not have any purpose in a poem?' Poetry is all I have, but who wants to read about these things in a poem? Poetry requires of you to think and feel at the same time, and very often to come to terms with your own poetic potential as a reader, and people do not like that any more. They prefer something they can relate to directly without getting involved." Nazareth felt, probably better than anyone, Mario's need to write about this torturous struggle with the real turned unreal, and vice versa, when reality becomes almost too "metaphoric" for poetry. "He's poised at the edge of a chasm of experience. He must find honest ways of naming it, courageous ways of incarnating it. He must be realistic in the process yet write poetry, which for him is the language of compression... He must find the language to do justice to his historical moment, that will dare to speak from within the soul of darkness." ("Post... Word" to *Versus Exsul*.) For Mario that included his experience not only about the war but also his whole life. It took him many years to come to grips with his childhood years after WWII. Having been severely malnourished, gotten over the "rheumatic eruption" from the hours spent with his mother in the shelter, when his shins turned into open sores, and then the para-typhus, when, he remembered, his mother made bread dough and put it on his soles to bring his temperature down, the plastic operation on his upper lip, without anesthesia, when he got caught in the barbed wire, he was extremely susceptible to physical pain, which, during the war in Bosnia, was, in some strange way, complemented with an absolute mental pain. The latter had primarily to do with "recovering" the conflict of his family life—his father, a genius at his job but a debauchee, a drunkard, who would abuse him and his mother almost beyond belief; his mother, a deeply religious person whom Mario loved but whose moral values had a rather painful impact on people around her. And, in fact, none more than Mario, for his mother often went, when he was a teenager, on some revenge crusade to prove to herself that her son could be no different from his father. Mario would talk about these things with Nazareth; one of Nazareth's notes reads, "Mario 'recovering' the past, trying dismayingly to 'uncover' the present—paraphrasing him: sitting in the darkness of the cellar, I often thought about my mother, still alive but physically inaccessible to me, and I would come to a sad conclusion over and over again that she hated herself. And I would feel guilt. Did I tell you she used to dress me in girl's clothes when I was little, though never outside the house? I think she didn't want me, no matter how briefly, to resemble my father even physically. During those damp, stinking hours in the cellar it seemed to me as if I had done something wrong to those neighbors of mine who were now shooting at me. You know, what struck me even more was the thought that they were doing that not because they hated me but because, deep down, they must have hated themselves. Then, in one of Mario's typical abrupt turnabouts, he laughed and said, 'Blah-blah! I should have been a preacher; only then would something like this sound convincing to me as well."

Later on he bounced between his mother and his aunt so often that he felt he never had a real home. And when he had to accept exile, he found not only life to be pain ridden but his very survival as a poet. "All this has nothing to do with writing in another language," he wrote in a letter to Nazareth. "This is the question of being sane enough to relive something in any language." He needed help and support in this other world, which, of course, nobody would risk giving him, simply because it meant a complete immersion in his life as much as in his poetry. And his own understanding of that brought him to the edge. "I cannot sleep as a normal person," he writes on the margin of "Release." "I often do not know whether I'm asleep or just dreaming of being awake. Even Borges finds something like this more tolerable, 'Acaso sueño haber soñado.' Which of these sounds, movements, words do survive in a poem?" Till the very end I failed to grasp fully the seriousness of his state of being. I often convinced myself that his torment was a poetic gesture, to a large degree existentially irrational. Maybe the reason was that Mario constantly blurred, in his own life, the rationale of poetic and non-poetic reality. "I just want to die," he told me one day, a beautiful sunny day. "With some dignity. Not to be shot at, demeaned, depoeticized, treated as an alien." Why do you continue to write then, I asked him, trying to make him snap out of that mood. Because that will speed things up, he said. "The mind will exhaust itself, and that's it then." I cannot but think that he conceived "Signs" at that very moment, or, perhaps, was already testing that thought on me, though that could be precisely my failure to fathom him. He believed that his life, including the one in exile, was one big illusion (delusion, I think), and he wanted to see how real that illusion could be in his poems. Robert Karmon's comment on the previous manuscript comes to mind as a profound insight into Mario's struggle. "As if his own survival surprises him, he conjures up searing human portraits out of the indifference of war and history, turning the tragedy of his mother's anonymous passing or a woman senselessly murdered by a shrapnel while waiting on a water line into poignant epigrams, fleeting maxims, trying desperately to find a point in the pointlessness of fate and destiny." He also tended to blur the distinction between the poet's I in the poem, which is often highly personal, creating sometimes ambiguous references, as in "blue and purple legs" of a boy being carried to a bomb shelter, and the protagonist's I. I asked him, out of sheer curiosity, referring to "Blind Walk," "Did you really meet that blind woman at the airport?" He quipped, "Would that be a better poem for you if I said that I did, or did not?"

Should this help anyone get a better insight into his poetry? Probably not. Why did I do it then? Well, maybe the question is irrelevant now. If not, the answer could be he was there to bear witness to the viability of poetry; his poetry is here to bear witness to the very possibility of his existence.

Jozef Klem

About the Author

Born in Sarajevo, Mario Susko is a witness and survivor of the war in Bosnia. Wounded during a mortar attack, he left the city in March of 1993 and came to the US that November. He graduated in English from the University of Sarajevo and received his M.A. and Ph.D. from SUNY at Stony Brook in the 70s. Between 1970 and 1990 he edited and translated poetry by Theodore Roethke, e. e. cummings, fiction by Donald Barthelme and Saul Bellow; also, he translated fiction by Bernard Malamud, James Baldwin, E. L. Doctorow, James Dickey, William Styron, and Kurt Vonnegut, among others. He has published nineteen books of poems, two of them in the US, *Mothers, Shoes and Other Mortal Songs* and *Versus Exsul*, where he has lived half of his past thirty years. He is the recipient of several awards, including the Nassau Review Poetry Award, the "Nuove Lettere" International Prize for Poetry and Literature for *Mothers, Shoes and Other Mortal Songs* (I. C. I. in Napoli, Italy, published the Italian edition of the book in 2001), and the Tin Ujevic Award (Croatia) for *Versus Exsul*.

DATE DUE

PRINTED IN U.S.A.

GAYLORD